flowers
STYLE RECIPES

flowers
STYLE RECIPES

photography DAVID MATHESON

styling NICOLE SILLAPERE

text SAMANTHA MOSS

style consultant BRETT KLADNEY

executive editor CLAY IDE

A Fireside Book
Published by Simon & Schuster
New York   London   Toronto   Sydney

the natural luxury of flowers

Cut flowers are the ultimate decorating accessory, bringing the vivid beauty of nature to the comfort and warmth of home. Like furnishings and artwork, flowers introduce new elements of form, color, and texture to a space. Unlike these other items, however, flowers let you reinvent a room easily, affordably, and on a whim.

At Pottery Barn, we believe that ease and inspiration are the soul of style. We designed our *Style Recipes* books with the belief that your home can be a unique expression of who you are, changing and evolving along with you over time. We shoot all of our photography in real homes, often in one day, so our ideas must always be accessible and simple to accomplish. Every recipe in these pages is fun to make and easy to achieve. We hope that our floral creations will inspire you to come up with your own personal twists – or entirely new ideas altogether.

WELDON OWEN

Chief Executive Officer John Owen
President & Chief Operating Officer Terry Newell
Vice President, Publisher Roger Shaw
Vice President, International Sales Stuart Laurence

Creative Director Gaye Allen
Business Manager Richard Van Oosterhout
Associate Publisher Shawna Mullen
Senior Art Director Emma Boys
Managing Editor Sarah Lynch
Horticultural Consultant Rosemary McCreary
Production Director Chris Hemesath
Production Manager Todd Rechner
Color Manager Teri Bell
Photo Coordinator Elizabeth Lazich

Flowers Style Recipes was conceived and produced by
Weldon Owen Inc.
814 Montgomery Street, San Francisco, CA 94133
in collaboration with Pottery Barn
3250 Van Ness Avenue, San Francisco, CA 94109

Set in Praxis EF™ and Formata™

Color separations by International Color Services
Printed in Singapore by Tien Wah Press (Pte.) Ltd.

A WELDON OWEN PRODUCTION

Fireside
A Division of Simon & Schuster, Inc.
1230 Avenue of the Americas
New York, NY 10020

10 9 8 7 6 5 4 3 2 1

Library of Congress Cataloging-in-Publication data is available

ISBN-13: 978-1-4165-7099-8
ISBN-10:   1-4165-7099-3

ranunculus and roses (page 1); china asters, creeping roses, roses,
plume cockscombs (from left, page 2); ranunculus and ornamental
grass (page 5); lilies of the valley (right); roses, gerbera daisies,
solid asters (from left, pages 8–9); variegated ginger leaves, crested
cockscombs (pages 24–25); tulips (pages 56–57)

contents

AND TEXTURE AS YOU BEGIN selecting flowers

SELECTING FRESH FLOWERS OFFERS A CHANCE TO PLAY WITH COLORS THAT SURPRISE AND SHAPES THAT DELIGHT

Whether you're selecting a single sunflower for an earthenware jar or a bunch of peonies for a glass vase, knowing how to choose and prepare flowers is the key to creating beautiful, long-lasting arrangements.

Base your selections on shapes, colors, and textures that play off one another. The generous blooms of summer roses complement the slim, structural profile of freesia, for example. Some flowers are casual, others more formal. Dahlias, like those at right, are compact and have full, round shapes that bring a light note to displays; in contrast, calla lilies stand tall and straight for an effect that's graphic and sophisticated. Experiment with a balance of tall and short, or of full foliage and simple stems. Or, compose an arrangement using just a single type of flower: a bouquet of anemones bunched dramatically in a vase is not only easy to create, it also lets the blooms' distinctive beauty be fully appreciated.

FROM THE FLOWER MARKET TO THE GARDEN, LOOK FOR THE FRESHEST, HEALTHIEST FLOWERS YOU CAN FIND

Whether you're shopping at a supermarket, florist, or corner store, look for flowers with vivid colors and full, flexible petals. Fading colors and brown, dry edges are indications that flowers have not received enough water. Crumpled petals and bent or nicked stems are signs of mishandling. With the exception of farmers' or flower markets, florists generally receive shipments of flowers that are already at least a day old. For the freshest selection, ask your store when it stocks its flowers.

To extend the life of your display, disinfect containers before filling them with fresh water. Use a flower freshener, or add one teaspoon of bleach for every gallon (4l) of water. With a sharp knife or florist's shears, cut two inches (5 cm) off the bottom of each stem, steeply angling the cut. A good rule of thumb is to cut stems to one-and-a-half times the height of their container. Remove any leaves that sit below the water line. For woody varieties, like fuchsia or lilac, use a hammer to pound the bottom inch (2.5 cm) of the stems for maximum water absorption.

curly willow and black-eyed susans; blood flowers and curly willow; black-eyed susans, drumsticks, blood flowers, and curly willow (from left, opposite); chocolate cosmos (top); roses (bottom)

USE CONTRAST — ORNAMENTAL PEAR OR PUSSY WILLOW WITH DAHLIAS IN FULL BLOOM — TO ADD INTEREST AND DEPTH TO ARRANGEMENTS

BALANCE IS THE SECRET TO A SUCCESSFUL DISPLAY, NO MATTER WHAT FLOWER OR VASE YOU CHOOSE

Choose flowers that accentuate the size, shape, and color of their containers. Base your choices on where the flowers will be displayed, and specifically where they are in relation to the eye. Tall stems, like irises and ornamental grasses, are ideal for a coffee table or near a fireplace, while small vases of roses or lilies of the valley are a better choice for a centerpiece because they won't interfere with sight lines across the table.

A bouquet doesn't always have to contain lots of flowers. Large blooms, like those of peonies and mop-headed hydrangeas, and striking tropicals, like ginger and anthuriums, make an elegant statement when displayed alone or in small groups. With more delicate flowers, like cosmos or lilies of the valley, it takes a larger quantity and a well-chosen vase to achieve the same impact. Whether in a formal arrangement or a casual bouquet, using an odd number of blossoms is generally more pleasing to the eye, as is choosing an interesting blend of colors and forms.

rose 'Yves Piaget' (top); ornamental grass (middle);
lilies of the valley (bottom); anthuriums (opposite)

USE CREATIVE FLORAL COMBINATIONS TO ACCENT OR HIGHLIGHT A ROOM'S EXISTING COLOR PALETTE

Anyone who's been thrilled by a dahlia's vivid hue can attest to the power of color. In Victorian times, the varieties and colors of flowers conveyed complex social messages: a white lily signified purity, for example, but a yellow one meant playfulness. Today's language of flowers is more open to interpretation, but whether you're viewing the fiery red of scarlet peonies or the calming green of bells of Ireland, it's clear that color still speaks volumes.

As you select flowers, keep in mind that limiting your color palette allows each hue to be fully appreciated. Experiment with basic color combinations: primaries (blue, red, yellow), harmonies (blue and violet, orange and yellow, red and orange), complementary hues (blue and orange, red and green, yellow and violet), or single-color arrangements. You can also choose a single unifying element, such as the dark centers of poppies, gerbera daisies, and black-eyed Susans, and let that be the theme that ties together your display.

geranium leaves (top); dendrobium orchids (middle); coneflowers and calla lilies (bottom); strawflowers (opposite)

coordinated colors

IN LATE SUMMER AND EARLY FALL, WHEN THE VIBRANT HUES OF DAHLIAS AND ZINNIAS ARE AT THEIR PEAK, CREATE AN ARTFUL DISPLAY BY TINTING THE WATER IN THE VASES TO MATCH THE FLOWERS.

dahlias and zinnias in layered vases

12 dahlias (varieties here include 'Barbarossa,' 'Camano Sitka,' and 'Orange Sunset') • 12 zinnias • 5 rectangular vases • bleach • food coloring • paring knife

Choose different flowers all in a single color, gather a harmony of yellows, oranges, and reds, or mix and match complementary colors (such as yellow with purple or red with green).

Select zinnias that are completely open, and dahlias that have flexible petals and partially closed blossoms. If the dahlias start to wilt, remove the outer petals to keep them looking fresh. The deeper the water, the longer flowers will last, so angle stems in the vases for maximum submersion. In spring, try substituting tulips; in autumn, use chrysanthemums to create the same effect.

about dahlias

- There are nearly 30 species of dahlias, from tiny pompons to the showy 16-inch (40-cm) dinner-plate varieties.
- Dahlias wilt easily; remove any extra foliage or buds from the bottom of each stem to help the flowers last for up to five days.

one Sterilize the vases with a spritz of bleach before filling them with water. To prevent bacterial growth and prolong the flowers' life, add 2 tablespoons of mouthwash or other antibacterial additive.

two Mixing colors as you would paints, add several drops of food coloring to the water in each vessel. The color for each vase can either closely match or be harmonious with the hues of the flowers it holds.

three Using a kitchen whisk or other stirring tool, stir the food coloring into the water to gauge the saturation of color. Add a few drops of the same color or of other colors until you get the tint you want.

four Using a paring knife, cut each stem on an angle. Arrange the stems in the vases so that most of the stem is under water, which prolongs the life of the flower.

AND OTHER TECHNIQUES FOR arranging flowers

TAKE YOUR CUE FROM THE SIZE AND SHAPE
OF FLOWERS TO PLAY UP DRAMA AND GIVE
THE MOST STRIKING BLOOMS CENTER STAGE

The composition of any arrangement should be determined by the flowers themselves and should draw attention to their properties. If a tall stem leans, highlight that idiosyncrasy by allowing it to droop. If a bloom is large, pair it with subtle foliage that gives it center stage.

As you begin, visualize the overall shape you'd like to create. A curved display, like the roses at right, has a fan shape that rises from the container. In a triangular arrangement, flowers ascend to a peak and then descend over the sides of a bowl or compote. A multilevel arrangement packs flowers upright in a square or rectangular container.

To support an arrangement, use vase-filler stones, straight branches, or florist's wire. Or, rely on the flowers themselves for a natural-looking framework: place a few stems in a container, turn it, and add a few more; repeat until you have a maze of intertwining stems.

EQUIP A SPACE FOR FLOWER ARRANGING WITH THESE TOOLS AND ESSENTIALS, THEN JUST ADD INSPIRATION

Whether it's a dual-purpose space, like a kitchen counter, or a well-stocked backyard shed, a dedicated flower-arranging area is a luxury that's easy to achieve. Find a space with lots of light. You'll also need a sturdy, scratch-resistant, and waterproof surface, like a countertop or cutting board. A nearby sink works best, but a handy faucet or garden hose will do. Efficient storage – wall hooks, bins, and baskets to keep supplies and tools organized – is essential. Here is a list of basic supplies:

Tools: florist's knife, florist's shears, pruning shears, small hammer, watering can with narrow spout, mister, and gloves.

Supplies: flower preservatives, such as oasis; green and clear florist's tape; rose wire and stub wire; florist's foam; florist's glue; vase fillers, such as glass marbles, pebbles, aquarium sand, seashells, and beach glass; and raffia and ribbon.

Containers: large bin for cuttings, buckets and baskets in various sizes, bud vases, cylinder vase for tall flowers, trumpet vase for bouquets, low bowl, compote, and bubble vases.

FROM MUMS TO ROSES, BLOOMS FLOATED IN WATER WILL ARRANGE THEMSELVES, SINKING OR RISING ACCORDING TO THEIR WEIGHT

graceful centerpiece

IT'S EASY TO CREATE A DINNER-PARTY CENTERPIECE WITH A MODERN GLASS-PEBBLE TABLE RUNNER AND STATELY FLOWERS THAT DRESS UP THE TABLE BUT DON'T HIDE THE GUESTS FROM VIEW.

allium blooms and glass pebbles

19 stems of allium • 3 trumpet-shaped vases, 12-in (30-cm) diam • strips of cardboard • 2 glass decanters • 3 bags of glass pebbles • 6 magnifying paperweights

Fresh allium, from the same genus as onion and garlic, can be used to create unexpected arrangements. The large flower heads hold lots of water, which prevents them from wilting during the course of a dinner party. You can add water later, but this arrangement is most striking when the vases are left completely empty. If alliums are unavailable, sunflowers, gladiolus, or amaryllis will work as well. For variety, you can mimic the shape of the allium flower heads by wiring two carnation blooms together and scattering them along the table.

about alliums

• Most plentiful in summer, alliums will last for two or three days without water if they aren't exposed to heat or direct sun.

• Alliums can be pungent, so use very fresh blooms and place the flower heads on the table just before guests arrive.

One Cut the allium stalks to the same height and place them in the vases. Measure the space you'd like for a runner, and frame it on the table with strips of cardboard.

two Place the decanters and vases where you want them, then fill in the space with glass pebbles. Flatten the pebbles with your hands. Remove the cardboard strips.

three Cut a few of the alliums where the stem joins the bloom, and evenly scatter the flower heads among the vases and decanters along the center of the table.

four Set the magnifying paperweights atop place cards to mimic the spherical shape of the alliums. Pick off tiny allium blossoms to place beneath each weight.

single-flower displays

THE POLISHED LOOK OF MASSED ARRANGEMENTS BELIES THEIR
SIMPLICITY. SUPREMELY ADAPTABLE, THIS METHOD WORKS WELL WITH
SPRING BLOOMS, SUCH AS TULIPS, HYACINTHS, DAFFODILS, OR LILIES.

massed tulips

20 parrot tulips in a single color • glass vase, 10-in (25-cm) diam

• Select two bunches of tulips, all in a single color, choosing flowers with attractive stems and fresh, vibrant petals.

• Cut all flowers to the same length and wash the stems. Tulips can continue to grow up to four inches (10 cm) and will open toward a light source, so re-cutting may be necessary to keep the shape of your arrangement.

• Pack the tulips tightly into the vase, beginning with a large bunch in the center and working outward.

• If flowers bend or droop, you can often repair them with a pinprick just below the blossom.

clustered grape hyacinths

2 dozen grape hyacinths • 3 small clear-glass vases • votive candles

• Secure small bouquets of grape hyacinths with string and set them in small vases for a delicate arrangement.

• Intersperse the vases with votive candles or objects that complement both the scent and color of the flowers.

layered arrangements

FLOWERS WITH LARGE, SPHERICAL HEADS GIVE AN ARRANGEMENT VOLUME AND SHAPE. CONTRAST ROUNDED AND CONICAL FLOWERS IN LIGHT AND DARK COLORS TO EMPHASIZE THE SHAPE OF EACH.

hydrangeas with horsetail

**12 blue mop-headed hydrangeas •
4 lengths of horsetail**

- For a modern effect, bend 30-inch (75-cm) lengths of horsetail between the striped joints and tuck these geometric shapes here and there in a mound of hydrangeas.
- Horsetail holds the bent shape because it's hollow. If horsetail is unavailable, substitute steel grass or bear grass.

peegee and mop-headed hydrangeas

**10 white peegee hydrangeas • 10 blue mop-headed hydrangeas •
ceramic vase • matches • alum**

- Prepare the hydrangeas by stripping the foliage from the lower stems and pounding the base of the stalks with a hammer, which will help the flowers take up water.

- Cut the tip of each woody stalk and singe it with a match to prolong the vase life of the flower. Alternatively, you can dip the cut end in alum, a pickling spice found in most grocery stores. Alum helps the plant take up water and last longer.

- Set enough blooms in the container to create a rounded base, then punctuate it by adding a few taller stems to each quadrant.

BRANCHES OF FLOWERING QUINCE CAN BE
FORCED INTO BLOOM BY BRINGING THEM
INDOORS IN WINTER, AFTER A COLD SPELL

flowers under glass

GIVE YOUR FAVORITE VASE A MODERN TWIST BY DISPLAYING IT INSIDE
A CLEAR CONTAINER, OR GIVE A SIMPLE BOUQUET A FRESH LOOK BY
SETTING FLOWERS BELOW THE RIM OF GLASS.

crested cockscombs

8 red crested cockscombs • 8 yellow cockscombs • ceramic vase,
12 in (30 cm) high • clear cylinder vase, 36 in (1 m) high • twine

- Cut the cockscombs using a florist's knife to make a clean, angled cut through the tough stems.

- Strip away all but the top leaves. Bind the stems together with twine to create a domed shape and a neat waist.

- Choose vases that allow enough room for air to circulate between them, or the life of the bouquet will be shortened.

- Dahlias and Sedum 'Autumn Joy' are good substitutes if you can't locate crested cockscomb.

yarrow in balloon vase

12 or more stems of yarrow • clear
balloon vase, 18 in (45 cm) high

- Cut the stems of yarrow to the same height, so that they measure just slightly less than the height of the vase.
- Balloon- or trumpet-shaped vases will work best for this arrangement. The flared shape keeps stems upright without crushing blooms.

tropical varieties

NATIVE TO WARM AND HUMID PARTS OF THE WORLD, TROPICAL
FLOWERS OFFER EXOTIC SHAPES AND BRILLIANT COLORS THAT
MAKE IT EASY TO CREATE ARRANGEMENTS FULL OF SURPRISE.

orchids and hydrangeas

1 spray of mokara orchids •
1 spray of dendrobium orchids •
2 annabelle hydrangeas •
ceramic vase • alum

• Prepare the hydrangea stems
by dipping the cut ends in alum
(see page 38). Arrange the
hydrangeas so that they cover
the top of the vase.
• Set the orchids between the
hydrangeas, letting their stems
fall toward the front of the vase.

orchids, proteas, and leucospermums

6 sprays of dendrobium orchids • 6 sprays of mokara orchids • 10 proteas
• 4 leucospermums • 3 stalks of seeded eucalyptus • 3 annabelle
hydrangeas • foxtail millet and lily grass as needed for filler • container,
10-in (25-cm) diam • florist's foam

• Soak orchids for ten minutes in room-temperature water before
arranging. Line the container with florist's foam and fill with water,
then remove any foliage that will sit below the water level.

• Begin at the outer edges of the container and create a base
with seeded eucalyptus, foxtail millet, lily grass, and hydrangea.

• Set stems of mokara and protea in the center of the container.
Follow the natural shape of each stem, and fill any gaps with lily
grass, eucalyptus, and foxtail millet.

seasonal centerpieces

CREATE A TABLETOP STILL LIFE THAT CAN BE SAVORED FOR A WHILE,
THEN EXCHANGED FOR SOMETHING NEW. GATHER FINDS FROM NATURE
OR REFLECT THE COLORS OF THE SEASON WITH FRESH BOTANICALS.

mosses and ornamental grasses

**trailing spike moss • pom pom moss • scirpus grass •
divided container, any size**

- For a flexible arrangement that's easy to refresh, choose a
divided container and fill the compartments with moss, grass,
or other botanicals. This display alternates rows (left to right)
of trailing spike moss, pom pom moss, and scirpus grass, but any
moss or grass will do. Aim for a mix of textures and plant heights.

- Line the container with plastic if it is not watertight, then set
clumps of grass and moss in each compartment. Use florist's
foam, cut to fit, if you need to create height.

- Water and mist frequently to keep moss green and fresh;
keep away from direct heat and strong light.

calla lilies and coneflowers

**16 dwarf calla lilies • 16 cone-
flowers • 5 bunches of kangaroo
paw • wine basket or other
divided container • votive candles**

- In the grid of a wine basket,
alternate votive candles and vases
filled with bunches of calla lilies,
kangaroo paw, and coneflowers.
- Bundle four to six lilies with
the same number of coneflowers.
Add two sprigs of kangaroo paw
and set in each vase.

SET LANTANA, LILIES, AND ALL YOUR FAVORITE
FRESH PICKS IN ANY WATERPROOF VESSEL,
FROM A JUICE GLASS TO A VODKA CHILLER

USE HANDPAINTED PAPER BAGS TO MAKE CENTERPIECES
THAT ENHANCE THE VIBRANT COLORS OF CHINA ASTERS,
ROSES, PLUME COCKSCOMBS, OR OTHER FAVORITE FLOWERS

scented arrangements

SWEETEN THE AIR OF ANY ROOM BY COMBINING FLOWERS TO CREATE A CUSTOM FRAGRANCE. THINK LIKE A PERFUMER, AND MIX DIFFERENT NOTES TO DESIGN YOUR OWN SIGNATURE SCENT.

geranium leaves

lemon geranium leaves • rose geranium leaves • 3 silver cups

• Many varieties of geraniums have leaves with scents as lovely as any flower. Try lemon, rose, nutmeg, or even chocolate geranium varieties.

• Keep the water fresh and leaves should last up to five days, although the scent will grow progressively more faint.

freesias, tuberoses, and lilies of the valley

3 freesias • 6 tuberoses • 9 lilies of the valley • 3 small silver vases

• If you love scents for the home, try going directly to the floral source. Tuberose, freesia, and lily of the valley are the signature fragrance notes in many fine perfumes, blending well to create a relaxing, romantic fragrance.

• Arrange single-flower bouquets in bud vases so you can easily blend different floral notes. Freesia, particularly white freesia, has a spicy scent that mixes well with the sweet notes of tuberose. The result is an earthy-floral combination that's readily available year-round. Change the intensity of the fragrance by increasing or decreasing the quantity of any of the flowers.

garden flower bouquets

RIBBON-WRAPPED SINGLE-FLOWER BOUQUETS CAN BECOME A COMBINATION OF CENTERPIECE AND PARTY FAVOR. THEY'RE EASY TO MAKE AND PERFECT FOR GUESTS TO TAKE AWAY AND ENJOY.

simple sweet peas

3 bunches of sweet peas • wide grosgrain ribbon, 18 in (45 cm) long • mason jar

• You can make a more casual bouquet by substituting a length of grosgrain ribbon for the satin streamers at right and using a mason jar instead of a vase.

• Separate any branching stems at the base to help with water uptake, then follow the steps at right for making a bouquet.

sweet peas dressed with satin ribbon

15 small bunches of sweet peas • 6 yd (5.5 m) of narrow satin ribbon • 3 vases • 3 elastic bands • florist's tape • 3 straight pins

• Divide the bunches of sweet peas equally for three bouquets. Strip the flowers from all but the top four inches (10 cm) of each stem. Gather 12 stems together and secure with an elastic band.

• Add stems in a spiral pattern, turning the bouquet and moving all the way around to get a uniform spherical shape at the top.

• Fasten the top and bottom of the bouquet with florist's tape. Bind with two yards (2 m) of ribbon: set the bottom of the bouquet in the middle of the ribbon, crisscross the ribbon upward, pin the ends into a flowerhead, and snip off any excess length.

SECRETS OF decorating with flowers

USE FLOWERS AND FOLIAGE AS VERSATILE ACCESSORIES, AND LET A WELL-CRAFTED DISPLAY REFRESH THE WHOLE ROOM

Flowers have the rare power to create atmosphere. With a little clever arranging, flowers can instantly change the look and feel of a space and make you want to spend time there. Even a few blossoms can refresh a room and decorate it to suit the season or a special occasion.

When accessorizing with flowers, keep in mind that the height and size of an arrangement should be scaled to a room's architecture — an oversize urn of snapdragons, for example, is best reserved for spaces with high ceilings. Take your cue from other items in the space: match the soft hues of a dining room with ranunculus, roses, and young bittersweet, like the bouquet at right. Gather inspiration from the paintings, fabrics, and colors in your home, and you'll soon see how flowers and their environment work together in a stylish partnership.

ADD THE PERFECT FINISHING
TOUCH WITH A FLORAL
ARRANGEMENT THAT TAKES
A STEP BEYOND TRADITION

Arrangements need not be confined to a table or shelf – in fact, you can be as creative with placement as you can with the flowers themselves. Use flowers and foliage to screen a fireplace, accent a windowsill, or decorate a staircase. As an alternative to a traditional arrangement, drape homemade flower garlands along an entryway or around a banister.

Experiment with the drama of single stems. Instead of one large-scale arrangement, divide a bouquet among a series of mismatched containers. Everyday objects – glass bottles, soup cans, teacups – take on surprising new character when used as vessels for flowers. Choose flowers whose color, shape, and fragrance complement the space or occasion. For added color and fragrance, incorporate fresh fruits and vegetables: asparagus, fig branches, and lemons are all versatile, long-lasting options that can anchor and accent an arrangement.

boxwood topiary, massed stock (left)

PINCUSHION FLOWERS IN A COLLECTION
OF ANTIQUE BOTTLES DRAW ATTENTION TO
THE SIMPLE BEAUTY OF EVERYDAY THINGS

flowers under water

SUSPEND ORCHIDS IN WATER TO ENHANCE THEIR MYSTERIOUS AND
EXOTIC BEAUTY. LIKE COLORFUL SEA FANS ON A CORAL REEF, THEY
RESPOND GRACEFULLY TO THE SLIGHTEST MOVEMENT OF WATER.

about orchids

- Orchids bruise easily, so check
them carefully before buying.
Branching sprays of orchids
will last longer if their stems
are separated at the base.
- There are more than 30,000
species of orchids. The most
commonly available are
cymbidium, dendrobium,
oncidium, and phalaenopsis.

anchored sprays of orchids

**4 sprays of phalaenopsis orchids • 4 glass pedestal vases, 16–20 in
(40–50 cm) high • 4 smooth, white river stones • monofilament**

Completely submerging wilted flowers in cool water for a few
hours will usually revive them, but why wait until blooms are
wilted? Magnify the color and beauty of orchids by securing them
to smooth river stones and suspending them beneath the surface
of water. Use several vases of different sizes, and add interest to
the display by placing whole sprays in some, just a few blossoms
in others. Measure the vases before you purchase the orchids, to
ensure that the sprays are long enough to fill the entire vessel.
Gloriosa lilies also work well in submerged arrangements.

one Pinch off any spent flowers, then cut the orchid spray so it is 2–3 inches (5–7.5 cm) shorter than the vase. Leave some sprays long and intact, and separate the largest blossoms from the others.

two Attach the orchids to the stones by knotting a length of monofilament around the stone and then tying the other end to the flower stem. Use a dot of florist's glue on the stones as needed.

three Fill the vases with water to about 3 inches (7.5 cm) from the top, then gently set the prepared flowers in the water with their stones. Be careful not to bruise the petals as you sink each spray of flowers.

four If desired, add more blooms or a few more stones at the base for interest. You can refresh the water without removing the flowers by carefully flushing the vases under a tap for a few minutes.

tabletop bouquets

LET THE CORNER GROCERY INSPIRE CLEVER ARRANGEMENTS FOR THE TABLE: PICK A BLOSSOM TO ACCENT YOUR COFFEE SERVICE, FILL A MASON JAR WITH LEMONS, OR REINVENT PRETTY CANS AS VASES.

tulips with queen anne's lace

18 tulips • 9 stems of queen anne's lace • 3 water glasses • 3 empty cans

- Cut the flowers to one-and-a-half times the height of the cans. If your local flower shop or grocery store sells flowers in ready-made bunches, you can use three bouquets in place of the tulips.

- Certain cans will rust, so it's best to set water-filled glasses inside the empty cans. Make sure that the glasses are hidden.

- Divide the tulips evenly among the cans. Add three stems of Queen Anne's lace to each can. Use extra tulip leaves to fill gaps.

- Tulips are ideal table flowers because they have little scent to interfere with the aromas of food.

nasturtium sprigs

nasturtiums • juice glass • étagère

- Juice glasses make charming vases if you've got a single flower or a broken stem, especially when displayed on an étagère.
- The vase life of nasturtiums is short, but their pretty leaves keep for a few days. Edible organic nasturtiums have a peppery taste that's a good addition to salads.

fruit and flower displays

CREATE AN ARRANGEMENT TO COMPLEMENT THE FRESH INGREDIENTS
OF A LUNCHEON MENU, WITH STALKS OF BABY ASPARAGUS AND TINY
CHAMPAGNE GRAPES TUCKED AMONG FRAGRANT ROSES.

ti leaf napkin rings

1 ti leaf • linen napkins •
florist's tape

- The large, pliable leaves of the
ti plant symbolize good fortune.
They can be cut for use as a
natural ribbon to secure the
flatware at each place setting.
- Cut a ti leaf into strips
1½ inches (4 cm) wide, wrap
around napkin-bundled cutlery,
and adhere with a small strip
of florist's tape.

roses, asparagus, and ti leaves

48 prince charles roses • 36 stalks of asparagus • 5 bunches
of champagne grapes • 1 ti leaf • cylinder vase, 10-in (25-cm) diam •
2 elastic bands • double-sided florist's tape

- Choose a vase that's at least five inches (13 cm) deep.
Stretch two elastic bands around the circumference of the vase.

- Trim the asparagus stalks and secure them under the elastic
bands, so they completely cover the container. Wrap a long strip
of double-sided tape around each elastic band. Cut the ti leaf
into long strips, 1½ inches (4 cm) wide, and affix to the tape.

- Fill the vase by setting the tallest roses in the middle and
working outward. Tuck clusters of grapes deep into the foliage.

BOUQUETS OF DAHLIAS, A FEW ORCHIDS, A SINGLE
HIBISCUS — CREATIVE FLOWER ARRANGEMENTS AT
EACH PLACE SETTING MAKE A TABLE LOOK SPECIAL

garden variety

CELEBRATE THE BOUNTY OF THE SEASON WITH AN ARRANGEMENT THAT
YOU CAN HARVEST STRAIGHT FROM THE GARDEN OR PUT TOGETHER
WITH GOODS FROM A FARMERS' MARKET OR CORNER GROCERY STORE.

hydrangeas and roses in melon

1 small melon • 10 annabelle hydrangeas • 24 roses

- Cut a small slice from the base of the melon to stabilize it.
Cut about two inches (5 cm) from the top to expose the flesh.
For a wide-mouth vase that will accommodate more flowers,
cut three inches (7.5 cm) or more from the top.

- Scoop out most of the flesh inside the melon and set the
vessel of your choice inside.

- Trim the woody stems of the hydrangeas and dip them
in alum (see page 38). Arrange the hydrangeas and roses
in clusters to create a nice rounded shape.

pumpkins and bittersweet

**2 orange pumpkins • 1 white
pumpkin • 4 gourds • 2 or more
bittersweet vines**

- Stack pumpkins and gourds of
all shapes, sizes, and colors on a
cake stand and tuck bittersweet
vines in between.
- Edible botanicals, such as curly
kale, rosemary, thyme, and fennel
flowers, also look good arranged
on a sideboard or dining table.

spring mantel displays

SOMETIMES IT'S THE VESSEL THAT INSPIRES THE FLOWER ARRANGEMENT, NOT THE OTHER WAY AROUND. GLASS-COVERED SERVING PLATES MAKE CLEVER SHOWCASES FOR SINGLE STEMS AND SMALL BOUQUETS.

freesias tied to paper

6 freesias • 2 sheets of letter-size card stock • twine

• For this modern take on Old Dutch flower portraits, punch holes through the sheets of card stock and bind the freesia stems to the front with twine.

• Freesia can scent a whole room in a few hours. Other flowers with opulent perfumes include stock, roses, jonquils, and jasmine.

tuberoses and tulips under glass

6 tuberoses • 1 tulip • 2 bud vases • 2 cake stands with clear-glass covers

• Instead of trying to match vase to flowers, borrow an old trick straight from the pantry: raid the good china and build your arrangement around the container.

• There's something especially wonderful about finding flowers in unexpected places. Instead of vases, try using a silver tea service, crystal ice bucket, or old-fashioned covered cake stand the next time you have flowers to arrange.

• A covered arrangement, like this bouquet of tuberose, has an added benefit in a dining room: floral fragrances can be contained during the meal, then released to scent the room after dinner.

DECORATE A HEARTH WITH CARNATION GARLANDS
IN SUMMER, AND BRIGHTEN IT WITH BITTERSWEET,
MAGNOLIA, AND OSAGE ORANGES IN WINTER

spa-bath bouquets

THE BATHROOM IS AN IDEAL LOCATION FOR AN ARRANGEMENT
WHOSE FOLIAGE YOU CAN USE TO SCENT THE BATH AND WHOSE
BEAUTY YOU CAN ENJOY DURING A LEISURELY SOAK.

roses, mint, and chocolate cosmos

20 garden roses • 6 bunches of fresh mint • 12 stems of chocolate
cosmos • rustproof rectangular vessel, 18 in (45 cm) long •
florist's foam • florist's tape

- Line the container with florist's foam and make a grid over the
top with florist's tape, or place three small vases in the container.

- Arrange the flowers so that they stand upright and cascade
toward the front, alternating mint with roses, then accenting with
cosmos. The effect should be similar to that of a window box, so
that the display is three-sided with just the suggestion of a back.

- Pick different aromatic plants for different seasons, such as
soothing lavender in spring and stimulating rosemary in autumn.

floating petals and leaves

1 handful of fragrant herbs •
1 handful of organic rose petals

- Essential oils from certain
flowers and herbs, like mint and
chamomile, can soothe the body
and calm the senses. Pick off
leaves from the herbs and add
them with rose petals to a bath.
- Organic garden roses have
the most scent and the least
pesticides, so choose them over
hothouse varieties.

guest-bath blossoms

WHETHER YOU HAVE BASKETS OF GARDEN FLOWERS OR JUST A FEW LEFTOVER BLOSSOMS, FLOATING THEM IN THE BATHTUB IS ONE OF THE EASIEST WAYS TO MAKE A BATH LUXURIOUS.

floating gardenias

• It takes more than 30 gardenias to make a single drop of perfume oil, but you can scent a guest bath or any other room in the house with just a handful of blossoms. The warm of bathwater releases the fragrance and essential oils of the flowers, creating a marvelously relaxing experience for the travel-weary.

massed gardenia blossoms

24 gardenias • decorative box or shallow bowl

• Look for gardenias that are mostly open but whose outer petals are still reaching upward. Set in a shallow box, with or without a lid, they make a fragrant welcome gift for guests.

• Gardenia is the top note in many expensive perfumes and was a favorite of jazz singer Billie Holliday. These fragrant tropical flowers are relatively fragile and will last only a few days in an arrangement, so the humid atmosphere of the bath is the perfect spot to keep them. Floating is also ideal for using short-stemmed, broken, or leftover blossoms from other arrangements.

FROM GIANT MONSTERA LEAVES TO SLENDER FLAX,
FOLIAGE OFTEN LASTS LONGER THAN FLOWERS,
AND LEAF FORMS ARE STRIKING AND GRAPHIC

festive holiday wreaths

VINE WREATHS HAVE A NATURAL CHARM YEAR-ROUND. THEY ARE
STURDY ENOUGH TO HOLD ORNAMENTS AND EVERGREENS, AND
THEIR FLEXIBLE FRAMEWORK IS IDEAL FOR FLOWERS AND BOTANICALS.

red amaryllis wreath

**30 silk amaryllis blossoms •
40 bunches of rose hips**

● Silk flowers are perfect
ornaments for the mantel, where
they're easy to see and unaffected
by the heat of the fireplace.

● The wreath shown above is
easy to make with silk amaryllis
blossoms and rose hips, using the
instructions at right, and simple
to customize with any colors.

amaryllis and rose hips with silver

**30 silk amaryllis blossoms • 20 bunches of rose hips • 30 silver
wreath ornaments • vine wreath • florist's wire**

● A woven vine or twig wreath makes a versatile base that
you can change with the seasons. For this project, you can
buy a ready-made base or weave grapevines in a circle.

● Cover the wreath with bunches of rose hips (readily available
at a florist), using twists of florist's wire to secure them firmly.

● Add silk amaryllis between each bunch of rose hips, pulling
the faux stems through to the back of the wreath and twisting
them around the base to secure. Insert silver ornaments by their
wire posts and affix them firmly to the wreath.

SIMPLE ART OF PAIRING vases and botanicals

USE SILK FLOWERS AND DRIED BOTANICALS TO CREATE LASTING DISPLAYS FOR EVERY SEASON

There's a world of alternatives to fresh flowers. Consider working with silk flowers, dried botanicals, and other organic objects, which are often-overlooked sources of exceptional texture and color. Instead of using fresh bouquets, try filling a vase with silk quill chrysanthemums, as shown here, or a trio of vases with stones and sea glass. Artfully arranged, these elements become long-lasting, high-impact displays.

Dried and silk flowers can be used again and again. The simplest technique for drying fresh flowers is to hang them upside down in a dry, dark place. This works best for sturdy botanicals, like cattail and heather. More delicate varieties, like daisies or iris, may require a drying agent, such as sand or silica gel. Silk flowers are often mistaken for real ones, and they have the advantage of requiring no care. Use them to create lasting displays on their own or to accent a fresh arrangement.

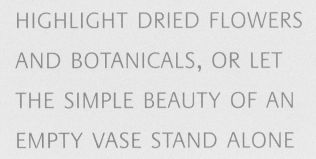

HIGHLIGHT DRIED FLOWERS AND BOTANICALS, OR LET THE SIMPLE BEAUTY OF AN EMPTY VASE STAND ALONE

Even without flowers, a beautiful vase can be a display in its own right. Vases and vessels come in many decorative forms, from hand-hewn wooden bowls to delicate porcelain teacups. There are, however, a few basic principles to keep in mind as you use them to create displays.

Choose a unifying theme and group objects by shape, color, texture, or provenance to ensure a cohesive look. For the greatest visual impact, display an odd number of items and arrange them asymmetrically. Whether it's a crystal compote or an enamelware bowl, the vessel you choose should highlight the objects it contains. Occasionally, forgo flowers and experiment with displays of dried fruits, botanicals (such as the cotton at left) and other finds from nature. Remember that repetition creates drama. When you work with a single color, the shapely beauty of a vase or the neutral tones of shells, stones, or dried leaves can be fully appreciated.

WITHOUT FLOWERS, A COLLECTION OF VASES
TAKES ON DISTINCTIVE CHARACTER AND ALLOWS
THE VIEWER TO FULLY APPRECIATE EACH PIECE

layered rose petals

ARRANGEMENTS OF PETALS HAVE A SOFTNESS THAT EVEN THE MOST
ROMANTIC BOUQUET CAN'T MATCH. MAKE A MODERN-LOOKING
CENTERPIECE THAT'S AN INDULGENCE TO ASSEMBLE.

about roses

• To tell if roses are fresh, look
for heads that are firm to the
touch and whose outer petals are
just beginning to open. Very firm
roses, with petals curved tightly
inward, may have been cut too
early and will be more difficult
to work with.

• Deeper-colored petals don't
show bruises as much and will
look fresher for longer.

rose petals in clear compotes

16 red roses • 16 coral roses • 16 yellow roses • 3 glass compotes

Capture the luxurious scent and velvety-soft texture of rose petals
by layering them in glass compotes. Petals from garden roses
typically have more scent than those grown in a hothouse, so
try to include some when creating this arrangement. When in
season, Oceania, Prince Charles, and Sterling roses are all good
choices to add scent and are readily available at a flower market
or florist. If you have a fading arrangement, use its petals to
create this display on a smaller scale, layering them in
champagne coupes or martini glasses.

one Cup the rose head in your hand and gently twist it from the stem. Once the petals are free of the stem, gently shake the loose stamens out of the center.

two Separate the larger petals until you reach the tightly curled petals at the heart of the bloom; set these aside. Keep petals of different hues in separate piles.

three Layer different color petals in glass compotes. For a finished look, make the deepest color the bottom layer of the first compote and the top layer of the last.

four Carefully add filtered water to fill each compote halfway. Petal arrangements will last up to four days – a bit longer if you completely submerge the petals in water.

seasonal vases

ONE OF THE BEST THINGS ABOUT AN INTERESTING VASE IS THE WAY ITS PERSONALITY CHANGES DEPENDING ON WHAT IT HOLDS. PLAY UP THE SHAPES AND COLORS OF FLOWERS, OR LET TEXTURE BE THE STAR.

summertime vase with dahlias

24 dahlias • 16-in (40-cm) diam container

● If you have a favorite quirky container, let it inspire a changing array of displays throughout the year. Covered in driftwood, this delightfully rustic vase makes a nice foil for dahlias.

● Vases with wide mouths require flowers that look good massed together. They also suit dried vines, either in a stand-alone arrangement or economically embellished week to week with a few fresh blooms. Narrow-neck vases suit tall flowers with multiple blossoms, such as lilies or freesias.

● To change the water but keep a bouquet in place, use a piece of twine to tie the arrangement snugly, just under the blossoms.

sea glass vase

sea glass • 6 white taper candles, 12 in (30 cm) high • florist's foam

● As an intriguing stand-in for flowers, pair a mound of green sea glass that you've collected all summer with several slim white tapers lashed in rope.

● If your vase is large, you may want to fill some of the space with florist's foam before adding a layer of sea glass.

silk arrangements

WHILE THERE MAY BE A GARDEN OF FLOWERS OUTSIDE, SOMETIMES THE CRAVING FOR THE RARE OR EXOTIC BEAUTY — ORCHIDS, LADY'S SLIPPERS, OR FRAGILE LILIES — CAN BE SATISFIED ONLY WITH SILKS.

checkerboard lilies

4 silk checkerboard lilies •
4 hanging wall vases

• Silk flowers not only fool the eye, they're also forgiving. Arranged high on a wall or left in full sun without water, they remain fresh and healthy-looking.

• The beautiful blossoms of checkerboard lilies have a musky, unpleasant scent, a drawback the silk versions don't share.

clematis and maple leaves

5 branches of silk maple leaves • 3 stems of silk clematis seedheads

• Use silk flowers and botanicals to create unusual and bold arrangements. Branches of red maple and clematis seedheads both have a wonderful texture, but they're not everyday items that can be found fresh at a flower shop.

• Silks have recently become so lifelike that it's nearly impossible to tell real from replica without touching the flowers. Rarely constructed completely of silk, modern fakes may contain chiffon, organza, velvet, paper, and even leather.

• Faux flowers are especially handy anywhere cut flowers won't thrive: use them to fill vases of clay or stone, which are porous materials that may contain elements harmful to fresh flowers.

stacked arrangements

RETHINK THE IDEA OF WHAT A FLORAL ARRANGEMENT SHOULD BE.
PAIR FLOWERS AND VASES IN INVENTIVE WAYS THAT HIGHLIGHT
THE BEGUILING QUALITIES OF BOTH PLANTS AND FOLIAGE.

gloriosa lilies with hydrangea petals

36 gloriosa lilies • 1 stem of annabelle hydrangea • 6 round clear-glass vases, 6-in (15-cm) diam

● Cut the lilies off the vine, leaving about three inches (7.5 cm) of stem. Separate the hydrangea blossoms from the stem.

● Fill the vases two-thirds full of water. Float two lily blossoms in each of the three bottom vases. To each of the top three vases, add a handful of hydrangea blossoms and ten lilies; turn the vase each time you add a lily to get a balanced display. Stack vases.

● Remove the lily stamens' tips to make flowers last longer. Lilies don't do well with flower preservatives or additives.

● If the flowers in the bottom vases keep sinking, cut a small circle of bubble wrap and thread the stems through the middle.

lilies with flax leaves

**36 gloriosa lilies • 2 flax leaves •
3 handfuls of chinaberries •
6 round clear-glass vases**

● For a variation, use flax leaves and chinaberries to add bands of color to the top vases.

● Divide the chinaberries among three vases and add water. Set 2-inch (5-cm) strips of flax leaves along the sides of the vases (the weight of the water will hold them in place) and add the lilies.

GLOSSARY

In this book, we refer to flowers by their most commonly known names. However, common names can sometimes be misleading as quite different plants may share the same name. To avoid confusion and help you identify plants at a flower shop or nursery, here's an alphabetical list of key plant names used in this book alongside their unique botanical name (in parentheses) and further information about the plant. Numbers in **bold** refer to the pages on which plant photos or information appear.

Allium (*Allium* species) These ornamental onions bloom in late spring and summer from bulbs planted in fall. *Allium giganteum* is the tallest species and bears dense, rounded, lilac blossoms, five inches (13 cm) across, of many, star-shaped flowers. **32–35**

Amaryllis (*Hippeastrum* hybrids) Large, showy trumpets — often four to a stem — are held on hollow but strong cylindrical stalks. Flowers are available in bicolors or in solid white, apricot, red, or pink. **33, 86–87**

Annabelle hydrangea (*Hydrangea arborescens* 'Annabelle') Apple-green, spherical flowerheads, which may be as large as one foot (30 cm) in diameter, turn white as they grow. **44–45, 74–75, 104–5**

Anthurium (*Anthurium* species) Dramatic and long-lasting flower spikes up to 18 inches (45 cm) tall consist of a flat, heart-shaped, glossy green or reddish spathe and an upright, cylindrical spadix. Species with bright pink or red spathes are called flamingo flower. **16–17**

Bear grass (*Xerophyllum tenax*) Thin and tough but graceful leaves may reach more than two feet (60 cm) in length. Florists provide bear grass in bundles of variable lengths and sizes. **38**

Bittersweet (*Celastrus scandens*) Woody vines bear clusters of tiny, yellowish-orange fruits that split open in fall to reveal bright red, decorative seeds. **58–59, 75, 78, 109**

Black-eyed Susan (*Rudbeckia hirta* hybrids) Golden rays and dark, cone-shaped centers make this annual wildflower a favorite in arrangements. Sturdy stems are one to three feet (30–90 cm) tall. **12–13, 18**

Blood flower (*Asclepias curassavica*) Clusters of vivid red flowers on three-foot (90-cm) stems bloom from summer to fall on a small shrub. 'Silky Gold' blossoms vary from yellow to yellow-orange. **12–13**

Boxwood (*Buxus sempervirens*) Boxwood's tidy foliage contrasts handsomely with floral bouquets. Indoor plants need bright light and a biannual trim in spring and summer to maintain their compact shape. **60–61**

Calla lily (*Zantedeschia* species) Majestic white flowers on long stems are most common. New dwarf hybrids are shorter, about 20 inches (50 cm) tall, and come in pastels and vivid hues. **10, 18, 47**

Carnation (*Dianthus caryophyllus*) All carnations have double, ruffly flowers. Garden varieties are bushy or dangle in hanging pots; greenhouse-raised florists' carnations have strong, tall stems. **33, 78**

Checkerboard lily (*Fritillaria meleagris*) Also called snake's head fritillary. The rectangular imprints on petals account for the common names. Garden-grown flowers droop slightly and emit a musky scent. **102**

China aster (*Callistephus chinensis* hybrids) This aster-like annual blooms all summer on strong, two-foot (60-cm) stems and makes an exceptional cut flower. Milady and Ostrich Plume hybrids have frilly flowerheads in white, pink, or purple. **2, 50**

Chinaberry (*Melia azedarach*) The small, bead-like seeds from the chinaberry tree are green in spring and summer, then turn soft yellow in fall. Keep chinaberries away from children and pets as they're poisonous. **105**

Chocolate cosmos (*Cosmos atrosanguineus*) Unlike pastel annual cosmos, reddish-brown flowers grow from a perennial tuber. Some noses detect a distinct chocolate fragrance, while others smell vanilla. **13, 80–81**

Chrysanthemum (*Chrysanthemum* hybrids) Hybrids include a dozen different forms, sizes, and petal shapes in a range of solid and mixed colors. See also spider mum and quill chrysanthemum. **21, 30, 90–91**

Clematis (*Clematis* species) Curved, silvery-gray seedheads follow lovely flowers on fast-growing vines. Because clematis have short, fragile stems, silk versions of seedheads are a more robust option. **102–3**

Coneflower (*Echinacea purpurea*) With its erect stems and pinkish-purple blossoms, coneflower is well suited to arrangements. To emphasize the prickly cone-shaped center, remove daisy-like petals. **18, 47**

Cotton (*Gossypium* species) Cotton balls dotted with seeds are harvested from fields in late summer and fall. Attractive dried bracts along the stem may be sharp. **92–93**

Crested cockscomb (*Celosia argentea* Cristata) Crested flowers are tightly clustered like velvety cauliflowers in shades of pink, bronze, red, salmon, white, or multicolors. Hang cockscombs upside down to air-dry for use in dried arrangements. **24–25, 42–43**

Curly willow (*Salix matsudana* 'Tortuosa') Twisty twigs create striking silhouettes indoors. When freshly cut, thin branchlets bend easily. Most willows are tan or yellowish green; *Salix* 'Flame' turns reddish-orange in winter. **12**

Cymbidium orchid (*Cymbidium* species) Grown outdoors year-round in mild climates, cymbidiums like cool conditions at night. Flower spikes may cascade or stand one to four feet (30 cm–1.2 m) tall. **64**

Dahlia (*Dahlia* hybrids) With strong, straight stems, attractive leaves, and blooms with a variety of shapes and petal patterns, dahlias are a popular choice for cut flowers. They come in an array of rich colors. **10–11, 14–15, 20–23, 43, 72–73, 100–101**

Dendrobium orchid (*Dendrobium* species) This orchid group produces spectacular, long-lasting blooms, in lilac, yellow-green, white, red, or blue, with a wide "lip" on the blossom face. **44–45, 64**

Drumsticks (*Craspedia globosa*) Densely clustered tiny blossoms form a rounded, mustard-yellow flowerhead an inch (2.5 cm) across atop two-foot (60-cm) fuzzy stems. They are attractive fresh or dried. **12**

Flax (*Phormium* species) Plants have long, pliable, sword-shaped leaves in shades of green, bronze, red, or yellow, many with contrasting stripes. **85, 105**

Flowering quince (*Chaenomeles* hybrids) White, coral, pink, or cherry-red flowers similar to apple blossoms appear on thorny shrubs in very early spring, usually before leaves emerge. Flowers are one to two inches (2.5–5 cm) across. **40–41**

Foxtail millet (*Setaria macrochaeta*) Use spike-like clusters of flowers either fresh or dried. To dry, hang bunches of flower stalks upside down. **44–45**

Freesia (*Freesia* hybrids) Highly scented, trumpet-shaped blossoms available in nearly every color endear freesias to gardeners. Florists' plants are treated to develop shorter, stronger stems. *Freesia lactea* has white flowers with a strong scent. **10, 52–53, 76, 101**

Gardenia (*Gardenia augusta*) Intense fragrance, showy flowers, and glossy leaves contribute to gardenia's appeal. **82–83**

Geranium (*Pelargonium* species) Scented geraniums vary in size as well as in blossom and leaf shape, but all grow readily in pots and offer heady aromas. **18, 52**

Gerbera daisy (*Gerbera jamesonii* hybrids) Stately solitary blooms with yellow centers are held on strong, cylindrical stems 12–18 inches (30–45 cm) tall. Hybrids have double rows of petals in radiant yellow, apricot, salmon, pink, or scarlet. **8–9, 18**

Gladiolus (*Gladiolus* hybrids) Gladioli grow from corms that bloom in spring and summer. For bouquets, cut floral spikes when half the buds have opened. **33**

Gloriosa lily (*Gloriosa superba*) 'Rothschildiana' is the most striking variety of this vining tropical plant, which is not a true lily. Scarlet flowers edged in yellow are four inches (10 cm) across. **64, 104–5**

Grape hyacinth (*Muscari* species) Bluish-purple or white flower spikes resembling hyacinths are borne on leafless stems. **37**

Hibiscus (*Hibiscus* species) These showy flowers are marked with prominent stamens and often a contrasting "eye" deep in the center of overlapping petals. They bloom in white, yellow, pink, blue, or red. **73**

Horsetail (*Equisetum hyemale*) Ancient, flowerless plants have scratchy stems with joints that resemble bamboo. **38**

Jasmine (*Jasminum* species) Jasmines grow mostly as vines. Most are white; not all are fragrant. *Jasminum officinale* is highly scented. **76**

Jonquil (*Narcissus jonquilla*) A spring-flowering daffodil produces clusters of very fragrant, golden flowers. **76**

Kangaroo paw (*Anigozanthos* species) This two-lipped, tubular flower from Australia, resembling a kangaroo's paw, is covered with fuzzy red, yellow, or green hairs. Blossoms on dwarf hybrids like 'Bush Baby' are two inches (5 cm) long. **47**

Lantana (*Lantana camara* hybrids) Tight clusters only two inches (5 cm) wide hold over a dozen tiny, tubular flowers on short stems. Most are pink, orange, red, or bicolored; 'Radiation' and 'Tangerine' blend yellow and red. **48**

Lavender (*Lavandula* species) Fragrant, tubular flowers are borne on long stalks on evergreen shrubs. Fragrance, hue, and size vary among dozens of cultivars. In warm climates, lavender blossoms in spring; elsewhere, aromatic stems bloom from summer through autumn. For dried arrangements, hang bunches to dry before the buds open. **81**

Leucospermum (*Leucospermum cordifolium*) Dramatic, long-lasting, orange to red flowerheads resembling pincushions, four inches (10 cm) across, decorate shrubs from winter through spring. **44–45**

Lily (*Lilium* hybrids) Trumpet-shaped white, yellow, pink, and red hybrid lilies that bloom in spring and early summer may lack fragrance. Those that bloom from summer to autumn are mostly white or pink, are highly fragrant, and may have upward curved petals with dark flecks. **48–49, 101**

Lily grass (*Liriope muscari*) Often grown as a grassy ground cover, arching, grass-like evergreen leaves form dense mats. Lily grass can be woven into bouquets. **44–45**

Lily of the valley (*Convallaria majalis*) Gather sweetly scented, dangling, white, bell-shaped flowers from woodlands or shady gardens in spring. 'Flore Pleno' has double blossoms; 'Prolificans' var. *rosea* is pale pink. **7, 16, 52–53**

Magnolia (*Magnolia* species) Magnolias have large, scented white, cream, or pink flowers. Small-leafed varieties of evergreen *Magnolia grandiflora* are best for indoor arrangements. Some deciduous species blossom before foliage emerges, and some have blossoms that shatter easily. **78–79**

Mint (*Mentha* species) Mints with large leaves, such as *Mentha spicata,* known as common mint or spearmint, are valued for their spicy flavor and aroma. **80–81**

Mokara orchid (hybrid from *Vanda, Arachnis,* and *Ascocentrum*) Delicate blossoms of this newly developed orchid are pink, blue, yellow, orange, or red and often covered with darker flecks. **44–45**

Monstera (*Monstera deliciosa* 'Variegata') Evergreen climber has pale, irregular markings on leaves, one to three feet (30–90 cm) long. Young leaves may be unbroken, but mature ones become perforated. **84–85**

Mop-headed hydrangea (*Hydrangea macrophylla*) Also called hortensias, mop-heads develop nearly spherical flowerheads. Pink flowers are most common, while blue flowers come from plants grown in strongly acidic soil. **38–39**

Mum See chrysanthemum.

Nasturtium (*Tropaeolum* species) In the garden, annual vines sprawl over ground or climb on a trellis, showing off red, orange, yellow, or salmon-pink blossoms. **69**

Oncidium orchid (*Oncidium* species) Flowers of both tall and miniature species have a prominent ruffly lip, and most are solid yellow or marked with brown. **64**

Ornamental pear (*Pyrus* species) Delicate pear blossoms decorate branches in spring; then, in summer and autumn, inedible, round fruits up to two inches (5 cm) in diameter appear. Tinted fruits show off best when leaves are stripped. **14**

Osage orange (*Maclura pomifera*) Hard, bumpy, yellowish-green, inedible fruits appear in summer on a tall tree that often grows in hedgerows. Skin contact with milky sap may cause a rash. **78–79**

Parrot tulip (*Tulipa* hybrids) This division of ruffly, feathery tulips often bears contrasting markings and stripes, typically white, pink, or blue, edged or blended with green. **36–37**

Peegee hydrangea (*Hydrangea paniculata* 'Grandiflora') Tight flowerheads of sterile white flowers range from 6 to 18 inches (15–45 cm) long. **38–39**

Phalaenopsis orchid (*Phalaenopsis* species) Most popular of all orchids, the moth orchids are either standard size or small-flowered miniature hybrids. Long-lasting blossoms in solids or patterns line arching stalks. Shades of white and pink are most common. **18, 64–67**

Pincushion flower (*Scabiosa* species) Pert blooms atop wiry stems show off domed centers. Lilac-blue is common, but there are also white, pink, and yellow varieties. **62–63**

Plume cockscomb (*Celosia argentea* Plumosa) Plumed cultivars have feathery, upright flowers in brilliant red, yellow, or orange. 'Fairy Fountains' blooms in a range of pastels including creamy-yellow and salmon-pink. **2, 50–51**

Pom pom moss (*Chamaecyparis lawsoniana* 'Minima Glauca') When very young, these conifers resemble mossy tufts similar to numerous true mosses that grow in woodlands or in shaded gardens. **46–47**

'Prince Charles' rose (*Rosa* 'Prince Charles') Smooth stems hold large blossoms, ranging from crimson to maroon, that take on a purplish hue as they fade. This large Bourbon rose blooms in summer on an arching shrub. **70–71, 96**

Protea (*Protea* species) Fresh or dried, flowers resembling thistles or cones hold their color and shape for weeks. **44–45**

Pussy willow (*Salix discolor*) Small tree produces attractive, silky, grayish catkins, about an inch (2.5 cm) long, on bare reddish-brown stems in spring. **14**

Queen Anne's lace (*Anthriscus sylvestris*) Loose clusters of tiny flowers look like fine lace atop stems with finely cut leaves. **68–69**

Quill chrysanthemum (*Chrysanthemum* hybrids) Fine, tubular rays with open tips on this fanciful, double-flowered mum look like soft porcupine quills. Quill chrysanthemums come in shades of yellow, bronze, red, white, or pink. **90–91**

Ranunculus (*Ranunculus asiaticus* hybrids) Thin stems may need support to hold extra-large flowerheads, such as Tecelote Giants, in arrangements. Cup-shaped blossoms may have single or tightly packed, double petals in orange, pink, yellow, or white. **1, 5, 58–59**

Rose (*Rosa* species) Cherished as garden and cut flowers, each species and variety has its own charm. In general, red and white roses yield the strongest scents. Fruits (rose hips) containing seeds develop from flowers as petals fade and drop; their shape and color vary, but most are red or orange. **1, 2, 8, 10, 13, 16, 27, 31, 50–51, 58–59, 70–71, 74–75, 76, 80–81, 86–87, 96–99**

Rosemary (*Rosmarinus officinalis*) Delicate lilac blossoms adorn thin branchlets lined with aromatic needle-like foliage. **75, 81**

Scirpus grass (*Isolepis cernua*, syn. *Scirpus cernuus*) Drooping, shiny, fine blades give this grass-like perennial one of its common names, fiber-optics plant. **46–47**

Sedum 'Autumn Joy' Easy-to-grow 'Autumn Joy' changes colors, chameleon-like, as flattened flowerheads on two-foot (60-cm) stalks brighten from green to pink in summer then turn reddish-bronze in fall. **43**

Seeded eucalyptus (*Eucalyptus cinerea*) Preserved or fresh, blue-green foliage has a spicy fragrance. Sprays of tiny seeds are valued for their decorative quality. **44**

Solid aster (x *Solidaster luteus*) Profuse clusters of tiny daisies decorate three-foot (90-cm) stems of this summer-blooming perennial. Blossoms are pale yellow with golden centers and make excellent cut flowers. **8–9**

Spider mum (*Chrysanthemum* hybrids) Narrow, tubular ray petals (florets) in irregular lengths give this chrysanthemum a graceful, yet spidery, appearance. Florets often have upturned, coiled tips. **30**

Steel grass (*Xanthorrhoea australis*) Long, thin, grass-like leaves, sometimes with slightly sharp edges, grow like giant pincushions in Australia. Spiky blades are stiffer than bear grass. **38**

Stock (*Matthiola incana* hybrids) Bouquets of this old-fashioned flower are highly perfumed and long-lasting. Hybrids have dense, 12-inch (30-cm) long heads of double flowers in vibrant hues of lilac, pink, rose, cream, or white. **60–61, 76**

Strawflower (*Helichrysum bracteatum*, syn. *Bracteantha bracteata*) Prized for their long-lasting quality, strawflowers should be dried before they fully open. Stiff red, yellow, pink, or white bracts circle a yellow center. **19**

Sunflower (*Helianthus annuus*) Plant pollen-free hybrids to use in arrangements. 'Pastiche' mixes reds and yellows; 'Velvet Queen' combines deep red and copper. **33**

Sweet pea (*Lathyrus* species) Modern hybrids have large, showy blossoms, but heirloom varieties are more fragrant. **54–55**

Ti plant (*Cordyline terminalis*) Sword-shaped leaves arch gracefully on stout canes. Named varieties, such as reddish-bronze 'Purple Tower,' have multicolored or striped leaves. **70–71**

Trailing spike moss (*Selaginella kraussiana*) Young tufts of this unusual fern look like mossy mounds. Trailing spike moss quickly spreads to make a distinctive base for indoor container plants. **46–47**

Tuberose (*Polianthes tuberosa*) Intoxicating fragrance fills a room or garden when pure white, spike-like clusters of blooms appear from bulbs in late summer. 'The Pearl' bears double blossoms, but single forms last longer. **52–53, 76–77**

Tulip (*Tulipa* hybrids) Tulips, which come in a wide range of colors, are divided into 15 groups based on blossom shape. Darwin hybrids are the most reliable to bloom in successive years. See also Parrot tulip. **21, 36–37, 56–57, 68–69, 76–77**

Variegated ginger leaf (*Alpinia zerumbet* 'Variegata') Beautifully patterned yellow and deep-green foliage upstages fragrant white blooms on this robust, tropical ginger. Shiny, lance-shaped leaves are five inches (13 cm) wide and two feet (60 cm) long. **24–25**

Yarrow (*Achillea millefolium*) Spreading mats of aromatic, finely cut foliage send up three-foot (90-cm) stems of flattened flowerheads four inches (10 cm) across in summer. Most are brightly colored in yellow, pink, red, or salmon. **43**

Zinnia (*Zinnia elegans*) Vivid colors of branching, single-stemmed annuals are fast-growing for cutting from late spring through fall. **20–23**

INDEX

ACKNOWLEDGMENTS

Copy Editors
Peter Cieply
Elizabeth Dougherty
Laurie Wertz

Designers
Adrienne Aquino
Madhavi Jagdish

Indexer
Ken DellaPenta

Photography Assistants
AJ Dickson
Tom Hood

Stylist Assistants
Julie Maldonado
Sara Mossman
Barbara Myers
Deneane Niebergall

Lead Merchandise Coordinator
Mario Serafin

Merchandise Coordinators
Darrell Coughlan
Scheffer Ely
Simon Snellgrove

Weldon Owen would like to thank the photography and editorial teams for producing this book and to acknowledge the following people and organizations for:

Allowing us to photograph their wonderful homes
Mark & Suzanne Darley, Charlie & Alexis Glavin, Brian & Jennifer Kelly, Nima Oberoi, and Greg & Amy Price

Supplying artworks
Woody Biggs (Paris Prints, Sausalito, CA)

Catering on location
Kass Kapsiak (Catering by Kass)

Providing assistance, advice, or support
Leonie Barrera, Angelica Biggs, Jay & Isabelle Dow, Rebecca Forée, Arin Hailey, Robert Hale and Gary Weiss at Ixia (San Francisco), Meghan Hildebrand, Linden Hynes, Rachel Ivey, Anjana Kacker, Anna Kasabian, Francine LaSala, Charlie Path, Michael Walters, and Colin Wheatland. Nicole Sillapere wishes to thank her family—John Betteo, daughters Anna and Nicoletta, Judy O'Brien, Sandra Schnelle, Kelly Schnelle, and Dawn Sillapere—for their love and patience, as well as talented team members Sara Mossman and Jennifer Stahle at Sillapere Events & Environments (San Francisco) and Jackson Chin at Dandelion (San Francisco).

All photography by David Matheson and floral styling by Nicole Sillapere, except for: Inside front cover and pages 8–9, 13 (top), 27, 30–31, 36, 48, 68–69, 72–73, 75, 77, 78 (left), styling by Nadine Bush. Pages 13 (bottom), 40–42, 92–93, photography by Prue Ruscoe and styling by Edward Peterson. Pages 43, 60–63, photography by Alan Williams and styling by Michael Walters. Page 45, styling by Ixia (San Francisco). Page 49, photography by Mark Lund and styling by Michael Walters. Pages 56–57, photography by Melanie Acevedo and styling by Anthony Albertus. Pages 76, 91, 94–95, photography by Alan Williams and styling by Deborah McLean. Page 78 (right), photography by Mark Lund and styling by John Costello. Page 85, photography by Hotze Eisma and styling by Anthony Albertus. Pages 88–89, photography by Stefano Massei and styling by Deborah McLean.